# This book belongs to

# Where is the Hedgehog?

# Written by Mairi McLeod

# Illustrated by Catherine Brown

Copyright December 2014
Mairi McLeod
All rights reserved

Where is the hedgehog?

Where can he be?

Where is the hedgehog?

He cannot be seen.

He closes his eyes and he dreams in his head.

 wonder when we'll see that hedgehog again.

Soon he'll be sleeping all through the day, until the winter has gone away.

When the children sing and come back out to play, maybe then we'll see that hedgehog again!

He's looking for a snug pile of logs and leaves,
a warm place to put his head down and sleep.
A hole in your fence- your neighbour's too,
not too big just enough for him to squeeze through.

As he snuffles and sniffs to his
warm winter home,
leave out food and water then leave him alone.
Shh, shh our little friend needs his rest.
Pick up litter to help look after your guest.

Gather the nuts and gather the seeds, gather the twigs and gather the leaves.

Soon I am sure he'll wake from his bed, when the sun comes out for the spring time again.

What does he need to keep him warm?

What does he need to keep him from harm?

**S**helter and food no wind by his bed,
when he wakes up he will be well fed.

A spiky ball curled up warm and dry, day and night he hears no animal cry.

He dreams of a time when the spring flowers come,
and he will wake up and the snow will be gone.

Gather the nuts and gather the seeds,

gather the twigs and gather the leaves.

Curl up in a ball until the spring time comes!

Oh look he's awake now the spring time has come.
In spring our hedgehog will come out at night,
in search of bugs, worms and slugs by the pale moonlight.

He'll drink lots of water to help him survive,
so happy now the warm spring has arrived.

So if you see a small hedgehog out in the frost,
you will know that the hedgehog may be quite lost.

Take him in, keep him quiet in a box safe from harm.
Then contact the experts and raise the alarm!

# Facts about Hedgehogs

1. A baby hedgehog is called a hoglet.

2. Hoglets are born in a nest.

3. There are usually 4 or 5 hoglets born to the same mother and this is called a litter of hoglets.

4. You may find hedgehogs nests under sheds, in piles of leaves or compost heaps – so be careful when tidying the garden or lighting bonfires!

5. If you find an injured hedgehog or baby hoglets they will need your help to survive.

Make sure they are warm and contact your nearest hedgehog support service.

There are many hedgehog support services in the UK including The British Hedgehog Preservation Society contact details below:

http://www.britishhedgehogs.org.uk/index.php

Here you will find useful information about what to do if you find a hedgehog.

# Outdoor Fun

Here are some ideas to try out at the park.

## The Sorting Box

Help our hedgehog find all he needs for hibernation by sorting out nuts, seeds, sticks and leaves and put them in a sorting box. An old shoe box with card across the length and width inside to separate the items will work.

# The Feely Box

Have fun with a feely box. We cut four holes in ours and had great fun trying to work out what we had found inside without looking. We found leaves, seeds, and sticks and stones too!

Great for learning new words and using your imagination too!

# Craft Fun

There are lots of ways to make your own hedgehog. We love the hedgehog handprint Idea!

## Hand Print Hedgehog Painting

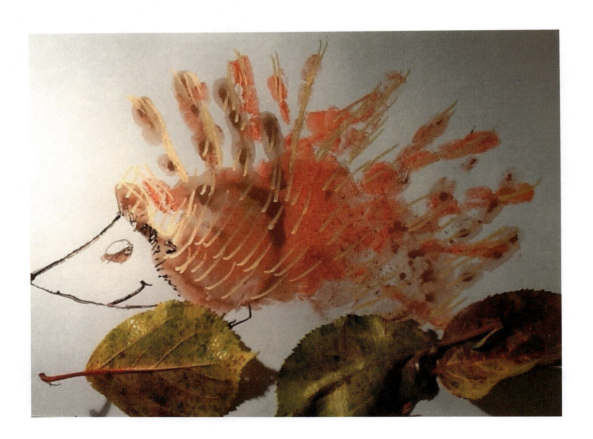

# Pinecone Hedgehog

And then there's the pinecone hedgehog. All you need is a pinecone, clay or plasticine and some googly eyes or even raisins!

# Acknowledgements

Thanks to the Families at Crane Park Children's Centre who started me on the hedgehog trail and Frances of FORCE (Friends of The River Crane Environment) who gave me opportunity to deliver the fun projects!

Special mention to my inspirational girls Kirsten and Lauren who are my best critics and guinea pigs.

Dedicated to my mum who passed on her love of poems and children's literature and who is always in our hearts.

Finally to Dave Mac – Thanks for the tunes!